CAMBRIDGE
UNIVERSITY PRESS

Coding
Club

Python:
Interactive
Adventures

supplemer

Chris Rof

CAMBRIDGE
UNIVERSITY PRESS

University Printing House, Cambridge CB2 8BS, United Kingdom

Cambridge University Press is part of the University of Cambridge.

It furthers the University's mission by disseminating knowledge in the pursuit of education, learning and research at the highest international levels of excellence.

Information on this title: education.cambridge.org

First published 2017

Printed in Malaysia by Vivar Printing

A catalogue record for this publication is available from the British Library

ISBN 978-1-316-63411-0 Paperback

Contents

Introduction

Who is this book for?

Python: Interactive Adventures is an alternative Level 2 book in the Coding Club series. You should either have read *Coding Club: Python Basics* before reading this or be familiar with Python 3 and have learnt about, at the very least, variables, while loops and if, elif and else statements. Level 2 is aimed at 12-13 year olds but is accessible to older children and even adults who want to learn about computer programming. Confident readers can choose which of the two Level 2 books they would like to work through before going on to Level 3. Many students however will want to consolidate their learning at this level by working through both books.

Why should you choose this book?

I want you, the reader, to learn not only how to make the programs in this book but also how to design your own. I want you to be able to write programs well, so that if you take it further and become the inventor of the next Google, you will not have to unlearn bad programming habits. This book explains important principles while helping you build short and useful projects.

What you need

Any flavour of computer can run Python 3. If yours does not already have it installed there is a section on the companion website (www.codingclub.co.uk) that guides you through installing it. This takes about five minutes! That is all you require to get started.

So that you do not have to do too much typing and so you do not get lost in the bigger projects, there are start files for all the projects in the book in one easily downloadable zip file, which also includes finished files, in case you need them. There are also answers to the puzzles and challenges.

How to use this book

You should read this book carefully and build all the main projects in order. At the end of each chapter there are further ideas, and challenges that you can think of as 'mini quests'. Some readers will want to work through them all so that they understand everything all the time. Some of you may prefer to rush through and get to the end. Which approach is best? At this level, it is definitely best to check your understanding by doing at least some of the ideas and challenges. If you are being guided by a teacher, to enable them to help you the most, you should trust their judgement.

There are four ways in which this book tries to help you learn:

1 By copying the code – this is important as it gets you to work through the code a line at a time (like computers do) and will help you remember the details in the future.
2 Finding and fixing errors – error messages in Python give you some clues as to what has gone wrong. Solving these problems yourself will help you to be a better programmer. In the end though, this should not become boring so if you get stuck the code can be downloaded from the companion website www.codingclub.co.uk.

3 Experimenting – feel free to experiment with the code you write. See what else you can make it do. If you try all the challenges, puzzles and ideas, and generally mess with the code, this will help you learn how to write code like a pro. Nothing is compulsory though. There are no exercises in this book.

4 Finally, this book not only provides the code to build some pretty cool, short projects – it also explains how the programs were designed. You can then use the same methods to design your own applications.

A word of warning

You may be tempted to simply get the code off the website instead of typing it yourself. If you do this you will probably find that you cannot remember how to write code so easily later. In this book you will only be asked to type small chunks of code at a time – remember that this will help you understand every detail of your programs.

Chapter 1
Data types

In this chapter you will:

- learn about data types

- learn about tuples, lists and dictionaries

- make a 'magic' card trick app.

Data types

In *Python Basics* you were introduced to **strings** (bits of text), **integers** (whole numbers) and **floats** (numbers with a decimal point). These are examples of **data types**. There are more! In this chapter we are going to look at some new data types: **tuples**, **lists** and **dictionaries**. These are all **containers** that store more than one piece of **data** but they do so in different ways and have their own advantages and disadvantages.

A string could also be included in this group as it stores a whole sequence of letters. We will find that there are several **functions** that we can use on strings that can also be used on tuples, lists and dictionaries.

Tuples

These are the simplest of our new data types. They can store strings, integers and other data types like this:

```
my_tuple = ("one", "two", "three", "four")
```

```
Python 3.4.2 Shell                                                  _ □ ✕

File  Edit  Shell  Debug  Options  Windows  Help

Python 3.4.2 (default, Oct 19 2014, 13:31:11)
[GCC 4.2.1 on linux
Type "copyright", "credits" or "license()" for more information.
>>>
>>> my_tuple = ("one", "two", "three", "four")
>>> print(my_tuple[0])
one
>>> print(my_tuple[1])
two
>>> print(my_tuple[2])
three
>>> print(my_tuple[3])
four
>>>
                                                        Ln: 13 Col: 4
```

Each **value** in the tuple has an **index** starting from 0, so `print(my_tuple[1])` produces the **output** two.

Unlike the other Python container data types we will see, the contents of a tuple cannot be changed after it has been created.

Think of a card

A common group of items that could be stored in a tuple is a pack of cards. There are 52 unchanging cards in a standard pack. It is often easier to handle the cards in our apps if we store the two possible characteristics of each card in two tuples:

```
suit = ("clubs", "diamonds", "hearts", "spades")
rank = ("two", "three", "four", "five", "six", "seven", "eight", "nine", "ten",
        "jack", "queen", "king", "ace")
```

The suits are referenced by their indexes starting from zero. "clubs" is stored in the `suit` tuple at index `0` and referenced by `suit[0]`. The rank of "queen" is stored in `rank[10]`.

? Quick Quiz 1.1

Which card has the two characteristics `suit[2]` and `rank[5]`?
1 The five of diamonds.
2 The six of diamonds.
3 The six of hearts.
4 The seven of hearts.

To select a random suit we can import the `random` **module** and then select a number between 0 and 3 using this code:

```
random.randint(0, 3)
```

and then use this in place of the index in the `suit` tuple like this:

```
my_random_suit = suit[random.randint(0, 3)]
```

What would be the code required to select a random rank?

You are probably familiar with selecting random integers in this way from Coding Club Level 1 books. The random module has a more reliable and convenient method for selecting item values in containers, `choice()`. Instead of using `randint()` to select a random suit from `suit()` we can use this code:

```
my_random_suit = random.choice(suit)
```

This can form the basis of many card-playing games or even the short app in Code Box 1.1. We are now going to work in **script mode**. Copy this code into a new **script** and try running it.

Code Box 1.1

```python
# thinkOfACard.py

import random

# Initialise variables
guess = ""
correct = "n"

# Initialise tuples
suit = ("clubs", "diamonds", "hearts", "spades")
rank = ("two", "three", "four", "five", "six", "seven", "eight",
        "nine", "ten", "jack", "queen", "king", "ace")
```

(continues on the next page)

```python
# Function
def choose_card():
    # Computer picks a card:
    guess_suit = random.choice(suit)
    guess_rank = random.choice(rank)
    guess = guess_rank + " of " + guess_suit
    return guess

# Start the game
print("Hello, my name is Mighty Persistent.")
print("I have magic powers: I can guess what you are thinking.")
print("Think of a card but do not tell me what it is.\n")

input("Press ENTER when you have thought of a card.")

print("\nYou are thinking of the", choose_card())
correct = input("Am I correct? (y/n)")

while correct != "y":
    print("\nOh, then it must be the", choose_card())
    correct = input("Am I correct? (y/n)")

# Finish
print("\nYay!\nI told you I could guess what you are thinking.")

# Exit nicely
input("\n\nPress the ENTER key to finish.")
```

Analysis of Code Box 1.1

OK, it is not the most sensible app! Now that we have that out of the way, let's look at what it does:

The import statement

We are going to use a **function** from Python's random **module** so we need to import it.

The tuples

We have to separate the strings in the tuples with commas. Starting a new line between the values in our container data types makes no difference, so we can use this feature to make our tuples more readable.

The choice () function

```
guess_suit = random.choice(suit)
```

This line of code asks the `choice()` **method** in the random module to select a random value from the `suit` tuple. The suit that is chosen is then stored in the **variable** called `guess_suit`.

Adding strings

```
guess = guess_rank + "of" + guess_suit
```

Remember how strings can be joined with the + **operator**.

This app kept my little brother occupied for hours!

? **Quick Quiz 1.3**

Read this code:

```
guess_rank = "three"
guess_suit = "diamonds"
guess = guess_rank + " of " + guess_suit
```

What will the variable `guess` contain?

The input () function

The input() function listens to the keyboard entry and waits for the **return** key to be pressed. It then returns the keyboard input as a string, which we can store in a variable just as we did when we stored y or n in the variable correct.

While loops

The code in a **while loop** keeps repeating until a certain test is successful. In this case the test requires correct to have the value "y".

Lists

A **list** is another type of container data type. These are very similar to tuples except that they can be altered. Think of tuples as quick, memory-efficient lists that cannot be altered by other code. We cannot insert or delete items in tuples with our programs. We can, however, use functions to insert or delete items in lists.

Lists are written like this:

```
my_list = ["one", "two", "three", "four"]
```

Just as with tuples, each value in the list has an index starting from 0 and the values are separated by commas.

Look at how this works in **interactive mode**:

```
>>> my_list = ["one", "two", "three", "four"]
>>> my_list[2]
'three'
>>> my_tuple = ("one", "two", "three", "four")
>>> my_tuple[2]
'three'
>>>
```

Hmm, the list of strings is surrounded by square brackets this time.

Do you remember that interactive mode in Python means using the Python **shell** rather than saving and running a file? It is very useful for running little experiments.

You can see that both a list and a tuple provide the same output. So, when would we use a list instead of a tuple? We would choose a list rather than a tuple if we want our program to add, remove or change an item within the list.

❓ Quick Quiz 1.4

For each of the following say which is the best choice, a list or a tuple:
1 A place to store twelve strings consisting of the months in a year (e.g. "March") that we want to use in an application.
2 A place to store names of the cards in a player's hand in a card game application.
3 A place to store the names of the compass buttons (N, S, E, W, NE, SE, SW and NW) used in a game app.

Dictionaries

The last of our container data types is a **dictionary**. Dictionaries take a slightly different form. In dictionaries we supply our own indexes. This time, we call the index a **key**. Keys can be strings, integers, floats or even tuples. Here are two examples:

key   value

```
my_dictionary = {1:"cat", 2:"dog", 3:"horse", 4:"fish"}
```

or

key   value

```
my_dictionary = {"1":"cat", "2":"dog", "3":"horse", "4":"fish"}
```

How embarrassing, I was confused for a moment here – I had forgotten that strings always appear in speech marks and numbers do not. So 1 is an integer but "1" is a number stored as a string!

No need to be embarrassed! We all forget simple things when focusing on new ideas. This is why it is so important to consolidate your learning by writing and experimenting with code. For this reason it is a good idea to make sure you try as many of the ideas and challenges at the end of the chapters in this book as possible.

Look at how this works in interactive mode:

```
>>> my_dictionary = {1:"one", 2:"two", 3:"three", 4:"four"}
>>> my_dictionary[2]
'two'
>>> my_dictionary = {"1":"one", "2":"two", "3":"three", "4":"four"}
>>> my_dictionary["2"]
'two'
```

Interactive Session

Dictionaries are unordered.

Try entering these two lines of code in interactive mode and see what happens when you press return.

```
>>> my_dictionary = {"1":"one", "2":"two", "3":"three", "4":"four"}
>>> print(my_dictionary)
```

Is the output in a logical order?

What's with the brackets?

When we create a new container variable, Python provides us with a quick way of defining which kind we require by the bracket choice:

- If you want a tuple – wrap it in round brackets.
- If you want a list – use square brackets.
- If it's a dictionary you are after – use curly brackets.

What's the difference?

Strings, tuples and lists are all indexed **ordered containers**; the values are automatically given an index based on the order in which they were input. Dictionaries have keys that *you* provide and the key-value pairs are *not* stored in any particular order. Strings and tuples have their content set at creation and cannot be changed by a program directly. Lists and dictionaries are containers in which values can be added and changed in a variety of ways.

It is also possible to create empty containers like this:

```
my_string = ""
my_tuple = ()
my_list = []
my_dictionary = {}
```

Useful functions

Table 1.1 provides a list of useful functions you can use on strings, tuples, lists and dictionaries. You can also find it in the Appendix. The table assumes the following containers have been created:

```
>>> s = "bar" # a string
>>> t = ("b", "a", "r") # a tuple
>>> l = ["b", "a", "r"] # a list
>>> d = {1:"b", 2:"a", 3:"r"} # a dictionary
```

Method	Strings	Tuples	Lists	Dictionaries
print all	```>>> print(s)``` bar	```>>> print(t)``` ('b', 'a', 'r')	```>>> print(l)``` ['b', 'a', 'r']	```>>> print(d)``` {1: 'b', 2: 'a', 3: 'r'}
print element	```>>> print(s[2])``` r	```>>> print(t[2])``` r	```>>> print(l[2])``` r	```>>> print(d[2])``` a

combine	```>>> a=s+"f"```
	 ```>>> a```
	 'barf'
		```>>> a=t+("f",)```
		 ```>>> a```
		 ('b', 'a', 'r', 'f')
			```>>> a=l+["f"]```
			 ```>>> a```
			 ['b', 'a', 'r', 'f']	

add an element			```>>> l.append("f")```
			 ```>>> l```
			 ['b', 'a', 'r', 'f']
				```>>> d[4]="f"```
				 ```>>> d[4]```
				 'f'

sort			```>>> l.sort()```
			 ```>>> l```
			 ['a', 'b', 'r']
				```>>> sorted(d)```
				 ['1', '2', '3']
				 ```>>> sorted(d.values())```
				 ['a', 'b', 'r']

delete an element			```>>> del l[1]```
			 ```>>> l```
			 ['b', 'r']
				```>>> del d[1]```
				 ```>>> i```
				 {2:'a', 3:'r'}

replace element			```>>> l[0]="c"```
			 ```>>> l```
			 ['c', 'a', 'r']
				```>>> d[1]="c"```
				 ```>>> print(d)```
				 {1: 'c', 2: 'a', 3: 'r'}

find	```>>> i.find("b")``` 0	```>>> t.index("b")``` 0	```>>> l.index("b")``` 0	
get length	```>>> len(s)``` 3	```>>> len(t)``` 3	```>>> len(l)``` 3	```>>> len(d)``` 3

Table 1.1 Some useful functions.

? Quick Quiz 1.5

For each of the following say whether to choose a tuple, a list, or a dictionary:

1 A container to store players, personal best scores achieved in a game app, such as: Jeff: 5400, Leela: 12600, etc.
2 A container to store the days in a week.
3 A container to store the monthly average temperature data for Manchester in 2013.
4 A container to store the names of the students who currently attend the climbing club.

Chapter summary

In this chapter you have:

- learnt more about data types.
- learnt about the container data types: tuples, lists and dictionaries.
- made a short 'magic' card game app.
- seen some of the different functions that can and cannot be used with the new data types.

We will explore these new data types further in this book. Here are just a few ideas that will help you refresh your coding skills from *Python Basics*. (As dictionaries are the hardest to use, we will wait until you have learnt a little bit more before providing any puzzles involving them.)

Puzzle

Write a new version of `thinkOfACard.py` using lists instead of tuples. It should work in exactly the same way if you get it right because lists can do everything tuples can and more.

Challenge 1

1 Add some code to `thinkOfACard.py` so that the computer, *Mighty Persistent*, says "Hi" and asks for the user's name at the start of the game.
2 It should then store the input in a variable such as `user_name`
3 Change the code so that the computer talks to the user using their name. At the end for example, it could say: "Thanks for playing [Name]. Please press the RETURN key to finish."

Challenge 2

The `thinkOfACard.py` app behaves oddly if the user types anything other than y or n. Add some code to catch unexpected keyboard entries and handle them a little more elegantly.

There are several ways to do these challenges.

To see some example answers go to http://www.codingclub.co.uk/book5_resources.php.

Idea 1

You could improve the `thinkOfACard.py` app by adding a tuple of silly comments that the computer randomly says instead of always saying: "Oh, then it must be the ..." such as:

```
silly_comments = ("I never give up, is it the ",
                  "I cannot believe I am wrong, it must be the ",
                  "Please let me try again. Is it the ",
                  "You must REALLY think about the card! Is it the ")
```

See if you can add something like this to your code.

Idea 2

Have a look at `guessMyCard.py` in the Chapter1 *Answers* folder and see if it inspires you to come up with some other funny card-based programs. (Note the use of `while True:` to create an infinite loop and the key word `break` to get out of it. This can be a very useful construct in game programming.)

Chapter 2
The Caesar machine

No doubt you will have heard of the Enigma machine used by the Germans in World War II. The encoded messages produced by it were said to be unbreakable. In this chapter we will build our own Caesar machine, which will not be quite so secure! It is, however, a quick fun project which will help us to see that **strings** are also **container data types**.

In this chapter you will learn how to:

- do modulus addition

- manipulate strings

- use for loops

- develop a simple algorithm

- turn an algorithm into Python code.

Strings are container data types too!

Let's just remind ourselves that strings are container data types with a quick interactive session:

Interactive Session

Open IDLE and type into the Shell window the following:

```
>>> my_string = "abcdefghij"
>>> print(my_string[5])
```

Now find out what letter is stored in index 0 (`my_string[0]`). We can do a couple of other things too. Try finding the length of the string with this code:

```
>>> len(my_string)
```

and then see how you can select a portion of a string like this:

```
>>> print(my_string[5:7])
```

This can be very useful but I think you might have found the result a bit unexpected. The first letter is not too surprising when we remember that a is selected with `my_string[0]` but the 7 indicates the first letter NOT to include.

Still in the same interactive session, try entering these code snippets to see what they do:

```
>>> print(my_string[:5])
>>> print(my_string[5:])
>>> print(my_string.find("b"))
```

Cool huh?

When we select sections of a string like this in Python, it is referred to as 'slicing'.

The Caesar cipher maker

Delving Deeper

Caesar ciphers

These are also known as shift ciphers. A shift cipher changes all the letters in a message to a new set of letters by shifting them a certain number, the shift key, to the right in the alphabet. For example, a shift of three would produce this cipher:

Plain alphabet:	a b c d e f g h i j k l m n o p q r s t u v w x y z
Cipher alphabet:	D E F G H I J K L M N O P Q R S T U V W X Y Z A B C

Open `caesarCipherMaker.py` from the *Start* folder found in the *Chapter2* folder. Check that this matches the code in Code Box 2.1.

Code Box 2.1

```
# caesarCipherMaker.py

# Initialise variables
alphabet = "abcdefghijklmnopqrstuvwxyz"

# Functions
def make_code():

# Get message
```

(continues on the next page)

```
# Change user input to lower case:

# Get cipher key

# Create coded message
```

This is a skeleton of what we would like to do. The interesting bit is going to be the **function**, so let's fill in all the other bits first. In your copy of caesarCipherMaker.py add the new code in Code Box 2.2.

Code Box 2.2

```
# caesarCipherMaker.py

# Initialise variables
alphabet = "abcdefghijklmnopqrstuvwxyz"

# Functions
def make_code():

# Get message
plain_text = input("Please enter your text to be encoded:\n")

# Change user input to lower case
plain_text = plain_text.lower()

# Get cipher key
cipher_key = int(input("Please enter a numerical key between 1 and 26:\n"))

# Create coded message
code_text = make_code(plain_text, cipher_key)
print("Here is your code:\n", code_text.upper())
```

Analysis of Code Box 2.2

Although this does not work yet, we have already sorted out how it will work. The user is greeted and asked to enter the message they want to encode and the cipher key they have chosen. These are collected into variables using the `input()` function. The program then prints out the encoded message that the user can send to their friend.

There are only a couple of things that should need explaining at this stage. When collecting the `cipher_key` from the user, the keyboard input has to be **cast** to an integer because the `input()` function collects all keyboard input as strings. This is done by wrapping the `input()` function in `int()`.

The `lower()` **method**, applied to the `plain_text` entered by the user, converts the string to lowercase. It is traditional when sending coded messages that the original message is all lowercase while the coded message is in all capitals. I am sure you can guess what the `upper()` method in the final print statement does!

Developing the algorithm

Instead of sliding two alphabets we can take advantage of the way Python stores strings. If the shift key is 3 then all we need to do is go through the message a letter at a time and output the letter from our alphabet string that has an index 3 more than the original letter.

Let's try and put that into a stepwise sequence. Remember we already have the `message` and the `cipher_key` stored in variables.

> Loop through every letter of the string message:
>> For each letter, find its index value in the alphabet string
>>
>> Add 3 to the index and find what letter this is
>>
>> Add the new letter to a new string `code_text`
>
> Return the `code_text`.

for loops

In Python Basics we learnt about **while loops**. Now it is time to meet **for loops**. A for loop is great when going through (**iterating** through) lists, dictionaries, tuples or strings. A Python for loop goes through a code block as many times as required. So in this case, once for each letter in `alphabet`. Study this **interactive session** to see how it works:

```
>>> mini_alphabet = "abcd"
>>> for letter in mini_alphabet:
        print(letter)
a
b
c
d
```

The orange words `for` and `in` are the Python keywords. `letter` is the variable we assign to keep track of all the items in this list. We could have called it `character`, `char` or `anything` (literally!). In some other programming languages a for loop is called a 'foreach' loop.

Now you have an **algorithm** and know how to construct a new kind of loop it is time to try and put them together. See if you can get the `make_code()` function to work a bit. Do not worry that it will fail in parts, we can sort out the problems later.

Hint: Start by creating an empty string to store the encoded message, for example, `code_text = ""`.

You will find an answer in Code Box 2.3.

Code Box 2.3

```python
def make_code(text, key):
    code_text = ""

    # loop through the letters and build the code text
    for letter in text:
        # add key to the index of the original letter
        i = alphabet.find(letter) + key

        # update the code text
        code_text = code_text + alphabet[i]

    return code_text
```

This is not perfect because our algorithm was not perfect! Sometimes you can imagine everything when building an algorithm, other times we need to tweak our code afterwards. Save and run `caesarCipherMaker.py` with this test data and see if you can identify at least two problems.

Test data:

Input	Expected output
Message = Abcd, cipher key = 4	EFGH
Message = abc123, cipher key = 4	EFG123
Message = wxyz, cipher key = 4	ABCD

Table 2.1

Have you identified two problems? One is that our function adds the cipher key but does not go back to the beginning when it reaches the end of the alphabet. The second is that it does not handle any characters that are not found in the string `alphabet`.

The second problem is easiest to solve. We must test to see if a character is in `alphabet` and then use an else clause for anything that is not a letter. What we want is to keep the actual character unchanged if it is not in `alphabet`. If you read back these last two sentences you can see how they almost sound like Python code. Compare them now with the amended code in Code Box 2.4.

Code Box 2.4

```python
def make_code(text, key):
    code_text = ""

    # loop through the letters and build the code text
    for letter in text:
        if letter in alphabet:
            # add key to the index of the original letter
            i = alphabet.find(letter) + key

            # using modulus addition update the code text
            code_text = code_text + alphabet[i % 26]

        else: # don't change the characters that are not in alphabet
            code_text = code_text + letter

    return code_text
```

The second problem is fixed using **modulus** addition as shown in Code Box 2.4. You can read more about this in the Delving Deeper box. For now amend your code and check that it works as expected with the test data provided in Table 2.1.

Delving Deeper

Modulus maths

This sounds really complicated doesn't it? Actually it is something very simple! There are some circumstances where we want to add numbers up to a point and then go back to the beginning, for example, when adding hours to a time. This is modulus addition. Modulus subtraction is going the other way. If it is 11 o'clock and we add 5 hours we want the time to be 4 o'clock not 16 o'clock. To achieve this we add 5 to 11 modulus 12 as there are 12 hours in a day. This is written in Python like this `(5+11) % 12`. Try it in interactive mode! The number of letters in `alphabet` is 26 so we use modulus 26 in our function.

> The modulus operator is %. This is the same operator that we used to find the remainder when doing integer division in Python Basics. I suspect this is not an accident... Have we simply added the hours together, divided by 12 and then found the remainder?!

The Caesar cipher decoder

OK, so we have some code that can create a coded message but our friend who receives the message wants some code to help her decode it. Although you will need to change the print statements a bit so that it makes sense, the functionality can be changed to decode rather than encode very easily, in fact only one character in the program needs changing! Save a copy of `caesarCipherMaker.py` as `caesarCipherDecoder.py`. Now in this new file see if you can find the one character in the code that needs changing. When you have changed it alter the print statements so that it makes sense. If you get stuck there is a working example of this file in the **Finish** folder in the **Chapter2** folder in the source code.

So, what was the character that needed changing? Did you spot that the key in the function needed to be subtracted from `alphabet.find(letter)` rather than added to it.

Chapter summary

In this chapter you have learnt how to:

- Do modulus addition
- Treat strings as container variables
- Use for loops
- Develop a simple algorithm
- Turn an algorithm into Python code.

The app is now complete, so here are a few ideas for **hacking** it:

Challenge 1

As `caesarCipherMaker.py` and `caesarCipherDecoder.py` are so similar it makes sense to combine them into a new app called `caesarCipherMachine.py` that does both jobs. To do this you need to ask the user for their message and then ask them whether they want to encode or decode it.

One possible solution is given in the Answers file that can be downloaded from the companion website: go to the dedicated pages for this book and then click the Resources link.

Challenge 2

Write a script that converts the time given in 12-hour time (e.g. 02.30 p.m.) to 24-hour time (e.g. 14:30)

Hint: Ask the user for the time in the exact format shown in the example so that you can easily chop up the string input (e.g. the first two characters are the hour).

Challenge 3

Write a script that converts the time given in the 24-hour format into 12-hour format.

Hint: Use the % operator.

Chapter 3
A simple ebook reader

In this chapter you are going to:

- learn more about loops

- learn more about tkinter widgets

- learn how to import text files into your applications

- build a simple GUI to control your ebook reader.

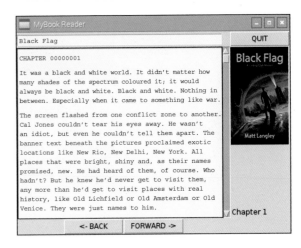

Designing and programming an interface

In this chapter you are going to build a simple ebook reader. This will include a graphical user interface or **GUI**, and require your app to import a text file. It is helpful to **decompose** this problem into a few smaller tasks. To start with we will just concentrate on building a simple interface.

You are going to build your GUI using Python's **tkinter** toolkit, which you should be familiar with from Level 1 books in the series. To recap, we do this in four stages:

1 Import the tkinter library.
2 Open a tkinter window where the main program is going to run.
3 Call the `mainloop()` method on our tkinter window at the end of our program.
4 Add the code to create the GUI widgets that are required in the window.

The `mainloop()` method continually checks for changes in the tkinter window and updates its contents as required. The code for the **widgets** we use must be placed **before** this method is called and after the code that creates the window. All the usual widgets found in professional applications are available for us to use. In this ebook app we are going to use a button, a text box, some labels and a scrolling text box. You can find some simple recipes for other tkinter widgets that you might want to include in your own apps in the Appendix.

Let's get started

Open `MyBookReader.py` from the *Start* folder found in the *Chapter3* folder of the source code. This has a skeleton for the **GUI** design laid out in comments. The first thing to do is set up the tkinter window code so you know where to put the code for your widgets. If you are feeling confident you can try and do this yourself or you can simply add the missing code from Code Box 3.1.

Code Box 3.1

```
#### MyBookReader.py

# Import libraries:
from tkinter import *

# Variables:

# Temporary variables to use until fully programmed

# Functions
```

(continues on the next page)

```
##### main:
window = Tk()
window.title("MyBook Reader")
# Create title textbox
# Add book title
# Create scrolling textbox
# Add text from first chapter
# Add the cover image in a label
# Add button
##### Run mainloop
window.mainloop()
```

If you run the code it should open an empty window.

It can be quite useful to have a quit button in an application. This requires two methods to be called: withdraw() to remove the window from view, and quit() to end the mainloop() releasing Python resources back to **IDLE**.

Add the code shown in Code Box 3.2 where indicated by the comment.

Code Box 3.2

```
# Functions
def quit_MyBook():
    window.withdraw()
    window.quit()
```

To call the function with a button widget, we pass its name to the command parameter. Copy the code in Code Box 3.3 to see how this is done.

Code Box 3.3

```
# Add button
button1 = Button(window, text="QUIT", width=10, command=quit_MyBook)
button1.grid(row=0, column=1)
```

The first new line of code in Code Box 3 creates a button of our design. We also need to place our widgets in the window, and this is done by the grid() method in the next line.

Delving Deeper

Building GUIs

Although all modern languages provide these GUI facilities they do not all do so in the same way as tkinter. When you are learning a new programming language and want to create an application, you will need to consult the documentation for that language to find out how it provides windows, canvasses, buttons, labels, etc.

The grid() method

tkinter's grid() method arranges its widgets in the window we have created with (row, column) coordinates starting from the top left (in common with most programming languages):

(0,0)	(0,1)	(0,2)
(1,0)	(1,1)	(1,2)
(2,0)	(2,1)	(2,2)

The window is divided into as many columns and rows as we require. Each row and column is numbered so that the cells can be referenced by coordinates in the usual computer science way: (0,0) from the top left. In addition to assigning a cell for our widgets, we can determine where we put them inside these cells by making them stick to the top (N for north), bottom (S for south), left (W for west) or right (E for east) of the cells. It is easier to see this in action.

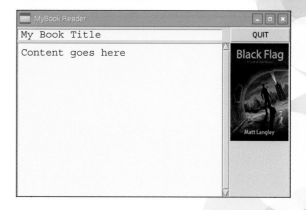

You are going to build an application with four tkinter widgets in a 2 × 2 grid.

In row=0 column=0 you will add a simple textbox for the title. In row=0 column=1 there is already a button widget. In row=1 column=0 you will add a scrolling textbox, and in row=1 column=1 you will add an empty label widget and then add an image to the empty label.

To access the image required you must have the **Library** folder in the same folder as the Python **script** you are working on. If you are working with MyBookReader.py in the **Start** folder for this chapter, as suggested, this will be the case. This application will import the text from a separate text file but for now you can just add some placeholder text in a few variables as shown in Code Box 3.4. Add this to MyBookReader.py now.

Code Box 3.4

```
# Variables:
textbox_width = 50
textbox_height = 20
paper_colour = "linen"

# Temporary variables to use until programmed
book_title = "MyBook Title"
book_content = "Content goes here"
image_path = "Library/Black Flag/cover.gif"
```

Rather than doing this a widget at a time, it is better if you add all the widgets at once so that, as you type them in, you can get an idea of how to create and manipulate any tkinter widget. The textbox where large amounts of text can be scrolled through is a special widget and needs an additional library to be imported at the top of the script. For now you will just add a simple label widget without an image. Copy the missing code from Code Box 3.5 into MyBookReader.py now.

Code Box 3.5

```python
# Import libraries:
from tkinter import *
from tkinter.scrolledtext import *

# Variables:
textbox_width = 50
textbox_height = 20
paper_colour = "linen"

# Temporary variables to use until fully programmed
book_title = "MyBook Title"
book_content = "Content goes here"
image_path = "Library/Black Flag/cover.gif"

# Functions
def quit_MyBook():
    window.withdraw()
    window.quit()

##### main:
window = Tk()
window.title("MyBook Reader")
```

(continues on the next page)

```python
# Create title textbox
title = Text(window, width=textbox_width, height=1, background=paper_colour)
title.grid(row=0, column=0, sticky=W)

# Add book title
title.insert(END, book_title)

# Create scrolling textbox
chapter_text = ScrolledText(window, width=textbox_width, height=textbox_height,
                            background=paper_colour, wrap=WORD)
chapter_text.grid(row=1, column=0, sticky=W)

# Add text from first chapter
chapter_text.insert(END, book_content)

# Add the cover image in a label
picture_label = Label(text="image")
picture_label.grid(row=1, column=1, sticky=N)

# Add button
button1 = Button(window, text="QUIT", width=10, command=quit_MyBook)
button1.grid(row=0, column=1)

##### Run mainloop
window.mainloop()
```

Inserting text in tkinter widgets

The `insert()` **method** used to add text to the two textboxes takes two **arguments**, a cursor position, which is usually an integer starting with 0, and the string to be added. The cursor position argument can also be the special tkinter constant `END`. This places the first character of the string at the end of any text already present in the textbox – in this case, because the textboxes are empty, the beginning!

Now it is time to run the script and check it all works before we add the book cover.

Adding an image to a label

First we need to import the image. We have already added its file path to a variable at the top of the script so this is relatively easy. Then we replace `"image"` with the variable name for this image.

Amend the label code so that your code now matches Code Box 3.6.

Code Box 3.6

```
# Add the cover image in a label
book_image = PhotoImage(file=image_path)
picture_label = Label(image=book_image)
picture_label.grid(row=1, column=1, sticky=N)
```

If you run your code now, you should see the cover image of *Black Flag*. Using the `Label()` **function** to add images to your applications is easy and can make them look very professional. That completes the GUI. Now to make it work.

Finishing off

A book reader should have some content. In the source code **Library** folder, you will find some text and a cover image for *Black Flag*. The text file contains the first three chapters from the exciting

Coding Club novel written by Matt Langley. To import a text file we need to know its **file path**, which is similar to that of the image. Then we need to use Python's `open()` function followed by the `read()` method. It is good practice to call the `close()` method after reading a file to free up the computer's resources. Putting this all together, we can now tidy up the beginning of `MyBookReader.py`. Amend your file so that it matches the code in Code Box 3.7.

It is really useful to know how to import text files in Python.

Code Box 3.7

```python
# Import libraries:
from tkinter import *
from tkinter.scrolledtext import *

# Variables:
textbox_width = 50
textbox_height = 20
paper_colour = "linen"

# Temporary variables to use until fully programmed
book_title = "Black Flag"
book_path = "Library/" + book_title + "/content.txt"
image_path = "Library/" + book_title + "/cover.gif"

file_in = open(book_path, encoding="utf-8")
book_content = file_in.read()
file_in.close()
```

Analysis of Code Box 3.7

Note how the **path** to the image and the text files are now constructed using the book title. This is so that if you need to change the book you simply need to alter `book_title`, which contains the name of the folder holding the book's resources. The `open()` method takes two arguments, the filename to be opened (and its path if it is not in the same folder) as a string, and an optional encoding argument. If you omit this your application might only be able read **ASCII** characters, depending on your operating system. Any accented or unusual characters will cause an error. Most text files in computers now use utf-8 encoding so, by including this argument, your book reader will be able to handle almost all text files.

The actual book title is stored in the variable `book_title` and the content of the book is stored in `book_content`.

You have now finished creating a simple ebook reader and it should enable you to read the first three chapters of *Black Flag*. Run your script and enjoy.

Taking things further

A book reader should be able to read more than one book. It would also be more pleasant to be able to read in chapters rather than to have to scroll for the complete length of the book. In this chapter's source code folder you will find a **Bonus** folder containing `MyBookReader2.py` and a library containing two books with their text split into chapters.

As you become a more accomplished coder, it becomes more and more useful to be able to read other programmers' code.

Delving Deeper

The Gutenberg project

Alice in Wonderland is taken from the Gutenberg project (www.gutenberg.org), which aims to make available to the public the text for all novels that are now out of copyright, including all the classics that are over 100 years old.

To make this work, it is necessary to be able to read directories, which is done differently by different operating systems. To accommodate this we import Python's `os` library, which handles the different ways of doing certain things on Windows, Mac or Linux computers. It is also necessary to create a few more functions and add a couple more buttons. To make everything look tidy another tkinter widget, the frame widget, is used. The frame widget allows us to add another grid inside a cell in the main window.

You should be able to open this file and see how all of these changes were accomplished. This is a bonus app; you are not expected to type all the code in. Don't forget to also have a look at the standard file structure used for the book resources. Can you see how to change your ebook reader code so that it works with *Alice in Wonderland*?

Chapter summary

In this chapter you have learnt how to:

- use tkinter's `mainloop()` to check and react to what is happening in your GUI apps
- add a variety of tkinter widgets to your apps
- import text files into your applications
- build a simple GUI to control your ebook reader.

Ideas

- Try changing the size of the text window in `MyBookReader2.py` to a size that suits your computer.
- Try changing the paper colour to something a little more daring than `"linen"`.
- Move the QUIT button to the bottom left of the reader.

Challenge 1

If you haven't already done so, amend `MyBookReader2.py` in the **Bonus** folder so that it shows the cover and text from *Alice in Wonderland*.

Challenge 2

Use what you have learnt in this chapter to make a GUI for `caesarCipherMachine.py` from the last chapter.

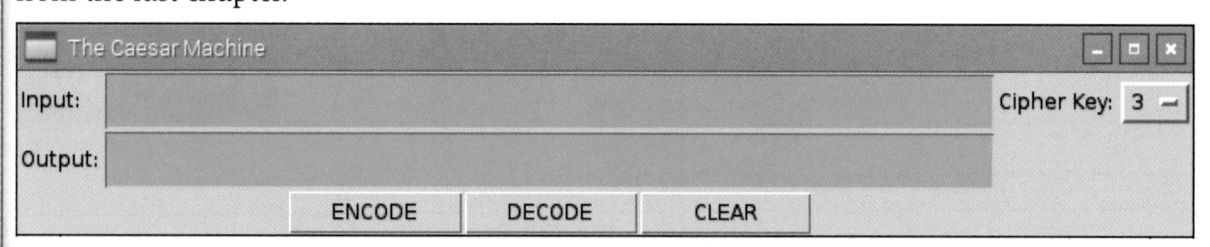

To help you, here is the code for the Cipher Key dropdown menu widget:

Code Box 3.8

```
# Create the cipher key dropdown:
options = tuple(range(1,27))
var = IntVar()
var.set("1") # initial value
dropdown = OptionMenu(window, var, *options, command=set_key)
dropdown.grid(row=0, column=3, sticky=E)
```

(There are recipes for this and other widgets in the Appendix.)

Chapter 4
An old-school adventure

In this chapter you are going to:

- make your own infinite game loop

- learn more about dictionaries, lists and tuples

- create a simple map for an adventure story

- learn how to make a simple text-based menu.

A long time ago...

This chapter starts the process of developing a sophisticated interactive story-telling app that you and your friends will be able to **hack** away at and make your own. We begin by creating a text-based adventure story similar to those that your parents played when they were your age. These games had massive maps that had to be navigated. There were items to collect and people to rescue, all using a few keyboard commands such as 'L' for look and 'S' for go south. They are great fun to write and allow you to practise and learn about the **containers** you were introduced to in Chapter 1.

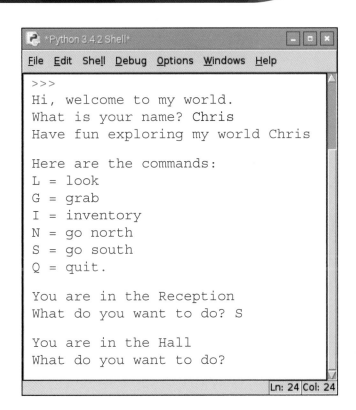

```
*Python 3.4.2 Shell*                    _ □ ✕
File  Edit  Shell  Debug  Options  Windows  Help
>>>
Hi, welcome to my world.
What is your name? Chris
Have fun exploring my world Chris

Here are the commands:
L = look
G = grab
I = inventory
N = go north
S = go south
Q = quit.

You are in the Reception
What do you want to do? S

You are in the Hall
What do you want to do?
                                    Ln: 24 Col: 24
```

All the work we do in this chapter will be built on later to make a story-telling app that's much more modern. If you cannot stand the suspense, you can open and run `mysteriousMystery.py` from the **Bonus** folder in the **Chapter7** folder of the source code now. This shows you where we are heading. It's a complete short adventure story and game that you can read and puzzle over any time you wish. If on the other hand you wish to enjoy the suspense, the journey and the excitement of discovery, leave this until you get to the Bonus section at the end of Chapter 7.

The first scene

For this project we are going to start with an empty **script**. All stories require a location so first we will build a simple menu and a location for our story.

Open a new script in IDLE, call it `rpg1.py` and save it into a new folder on your computer. Copy in the code from Code Box 4.1 and save again.

Code Box 4.1

```
# rpg1.py
#This game has one room

room = {"name": "Reception",
        "item": "mobile phone"}

backpack = []

# Functions
def look():
    pass

def grab():
    pass
```

(continues on the next page)

```
def inventory():
    pass

# Start game
name = input("Hi, welcome to my world.\nWhat is your name?")
print("Have fun exploring my world", name, "\n\nHere are the commands:")
print("L = look, G = grab, I = inventory, Q = quit.")

# Create infinite loop

# End game politely
print("\nThanks for playing", name)
```

Analysis of Code Box 4.1

Our scene is a room and it has a name and an item in it. As we add other rooms to our game they will also have names and maybe items and other things. This is an ideal time to use a **dictionary**, so we can look up the name and item using sensible **keys**. Here is an **interactive session** to remind you how this works:

```
>>> room = {"name": "Reception", "item": "mobile phone"}
>>> room["item"]
'mobile phone'
>>>
```

Note that in container data types, white space and line returns are ignored inside the brackets. We can take advantage of this to make our **scripts** easier to read as shown in Code Box 4.1.

Every adventurer needs a backpack to store their treasures. As these items can change, a **list** is best to store them in rather than a **tuple**. At the start of the adventure the backpack is empty, so we create an empty list with [].

The rest of the code should be familiar to you now.

Running this script is not very exciting yet but it shows how to start planning a game. We have asked for the user's name, greeted them and constructed a simple menu. We have made empty **functions** for the things the user will be able to do and used the Python keyword `pass` to allow the functions to be called but do nothing.

Decomposing complex problems into smaller parts is an important computational thinking skill. Identifying the need for and making empty functions is a useful way of keeping track of the tasks required to be completed, as is adding comments to indicate other jobs that are required.

Experiment

Try running the program after deleting `pass` from one of the functions to see why `pass` is needed.

By creating empty functions we have built an overview of our app and broken the problem down into smaller tasks that can be solved when we are ready.

Adding an infinite loop

If an infinite loop is good enough for tkinter ...

Making an **infinite loop** in Python is easy. We simply create a **while loop** that loops while `True`. This goes on forever. At some point we will want to break out of this loop – such as when the game is complete. To do this we use the `break` keyword. Add the code from Code Box 4.2 to your app to see how easy it is to set up a **game loop**.

```
Code Box 4.2                                              x

# Create infinite loop
while True:
    print("\nYou are in the", room["name"])
    command = input("What do you want to do?")
    if command == "L":
```

(continues on the next page)

```
            look()
        elif command == "G":
            grab()
        elif command == "I":
            inventory()
        elif command == "Q":
            break

# End game politely
print("\nThanks for playing", name)
```

This should all make perfect sense. The only command in the game that actually works when you run it is the "Q" command, which breaks out of the loop. The other commands call empty functions. The game still runs. Building it this way allows us to check our progress as we go along.

Adding functionality

The look() function should check to see if there is an item in the room and print out what the user can see or notify them that there is nothing to be seen.

The grab() function should look to see if there is an item in the room and then add it to the backpack and remove it from the room.

The inventory() function should print out all the items in the backpack.

See how many of these three functions you can write yourself. You may need to look back at Chapter 1 or the Appendix to see how to add and remove items from lists and dictionaries when writing the grab() function. One way of writing the three functions is given in Code Box 4.3. Did you come up with something better?

Code Box 4.3

```python
# Functions
def look():
    if "item" in room:
        print("You can see a " + room["item"])
    else:
        print("Nothing to see here.")

def grab():
    if "item" in room:
        backpack.append(room["item"])
        print("You now have the " + room["item"])
        del room["item"]
    else:
        print("Nothing to grab here.")

def inventory():
    print(backpack)
```

Adding more rooms

Although it is quite satisfying to look around the Reception room and put a mobile phone into your backpack, this game could definitely use more rooms! Save a copy of rpg1.py into the folder you are using for this chapter with the name rpg2.py

We are now going to add two more rooms to our game, so there will be three in total. We know that they can be created with a dictionary, but how should we store the rooms?

What is the best choice of container in which to store a group of dictionaries?
- A tuple.
- A list.
- Another dictionary.

There are sensible arguments for any of these choices. However since the rooms already have names there is no need to give them another unique **key** so perhaps not a dictionary. As we are not going to be adding and taking rooms away in our story (that would just be odd) the sensible choice would be a tuple. (Surprisingly, changing the contents of the dictionaries does not count as changing the tuple.)

Amend `rpg2.py` so that it has all the information required for the three rooms in a tuple of dictionaries as shown in Code Box 4.4.

Code Box 4.4

```python
# rpg2.py
# This game has three rooms.
# The aim is to collect the phone and sim card.

rooms = (
    { "name": "Reception",
      "item": "mobile phone" },

    { "name": "Hall" },

    { "name": "Lounge",
      "item": "sim card" }
    )

backpack = []
```

Note how we have used white space and line returns to make the code easier to read.

We can now get information about our rooms like this:

```
print(rooms[2])
```
outputs:

```
{'item': 'sim card', 'name': 'Lounge'}
```

To print out the item in the reception we would use this code:

```
print(rooms[0]["item"])
```

which would output

```
mobile phone
```

Experiment

Using this new knowledge, can you alter the code in `rpg2.py` so that it works as it did before when there was only one room? Leave the rooms tuple of dictionaries as it now is. Your answer should ignore the two new rooms.

The answer can be found in the *Experiments* folder in the source code provided for this chapter.

Rewriting the functions to cope with three rooms

To keep track of which room is required we need a new variable to store a room's **index**. As we are starting the game in the Reception we can **initialise** `current_location` to 0 straight after `backpack`.

To print out the item in the Reception you would need to replace any zeros you just inserted in your experiment with the variable `current_location`, so

```
print(rooms[0]["item"])
```

becomes

```
print(rooms[current_location]["item"])
```

If you make these replacements in `rpg2.py` now, your game should still work in the same way as before and your code should look like that shown in Code Box 4.5.

Code Box 4.5

```
backpack = []
current_location = 0
# Functions
def look():
    if "item" in rooms[current_location]:
        print("You can see a " + rooms[current_location]["item"])
    else:
        print("Nothing to see here.")

def grab():
    if "item" in rooms[current_location]:
        backpack.append(rooms[current_location]["item"])
        print("You now have the " + rooms[current_location]["item"])
        del rooms[current_location]["item"]
    else:
        print("Nothing to grab here.")
```

(continues on the next page)

```python
def inventory():
    print(backpack)

# Start game
name = input("Hi, welcome to my world.\nWhat is your name?")
print("Have fun exploring my world", name, "\n\nHere are the commands:")
print("L = look, G = grab, I = inventory, Q = quit.")

# Create infinite loop:
while True:
    print("\nYou are in the", rooms[current_location]["name"])
    command = input("What do you want to do?")
    if command == "L":
        look()
    elif command == "G":
        grab()
    elif command == "I":
        inventory()
    elif command == "Q":
        break

# End game politely
print("\nThanks for playing", name)
```

Let's now add two more placeholder functions, move_north() and move_south(), and extend
the menu a little to accommodate these new functions. Add the code from Code Box 4.6 to rpg2.py
and then run it to check there are no errors. It should still behave just as before!

Code Box 4.6

```python
def move_north():
    pass

def move_south():
    pass

# Start game
name = input("Hi, welcome to my world.\nWhat is your name?")
print("Have fun exploring my world", name, "\n\nHere are the commands:")
print("L = look, G = grab, N = go north, S = go south, I = inventory, Q = quit.")
# Create infinite loop:
while True:
    print("\nYou are in the", rooms[current_location]["name"])
    command = input("What do you want to do?")
    if command == "L":
        look()
    elif command == "G":
        grab()
    elif command == "I":
        inventory()
    elif command == "N":
        move_north()
    elif command == "S":
        move_south()
    elif command == "Q":
        break
    else:
        print("\nPlease enter only L, G, I, N, S or Q")

print("\nThanks for playing", name)
```

This version is better as we are now catching any unexpected user input. It would be nice to allow lowercase commands as well. Can you amend the game loop to allow this? One possible answer is shown in Code Box 4.7.

Code Box 4.7

```
# Create infinite loop:
while True:
    print("\nYou are in the", rooms[current_location]["name"])
    command = input("What do you want to do?")
    if command == "L" or command == "l":
        look()
    elif command == "G" or command == "g":
        grab()
    elif command == "I" or command == "i":
        inventory()
    elif command == "N" or command == "n":
        move_north()
    elif command == "S" or command == "s":
        move_south()
    elif command == "Q" or command == "q":
        break
    else:
        print("\nPlease enter only L, G, I, N, S or Q")
```

Finally it is time to write the functions! Moving north involves decreasing the current_location by 1. Thus, as this is a **global variable**, we must re-declare it in the function before anything else. It is also important to check that this is possible with a simple test and provide some feedback to the user. If you are feeling confident, you may wish to write this function before looking at Code Box 4.8. If not, copy this code in and then try and write the move_south() function before looking at Code Box 4.9.

Code Box 4.8

```python
def move_north():
    global current_location
    if current_location > 0:
        current_location=current_location-1
    else:
        print("You have bumped into a wall.")
```

Delving Deeper

Global variables

A variable that is created (initialised) at the beginning of your program, outside of any function, is a global variable. A variable that is initialised inside a function is a **local variable**. In many of the programs you have built so far we have created a bunch of global variables at the beginning of our code. In fact they are usually constants that are not going to be changed by the program but might be changed by us to adjust some overall property. This group of variables behaves like a configuration file or a settings menu.

current_location is a global variable that is changed by the program in both the move_north() and move_south() scripts.

Many programmers discourage the use of global variables. This is because they are inherently dangerous: a function that alters a global variable could break any number of other functions that rely on it, thus making the code difficult to maintain and liable to cause problems. So in Python, when you want to change the value of a global variable in a function, you are forced to re-declare it with the keyword global. If you don't do this a new local variable with the same name is created.

Basically, Python is forcing you to say that you are aware that this is a global variable and that you accept all responsibility for changing it in this function!

Code Box 4.9

```python
def move_south():
    global current_location
    if current_location < 2:
        current_location=current_location+1
    else:
        print("You have bumped into a wall.")
```

If this app is going to have more rooms, it would be better if the move_south() function could work out where the end of the map is itself. We could use len() to find the length of the tuple and subtract 1. The code would then look like Code Box 4.10.

Code Box 4.10

```python
def move_south():
    global current_location
    if current_location < len(rooms)-1:
        current_location=current_location+1
    else:
        print("You have bumped into a wall.")
```

? Quick Quiz 4.2

Why is it necessary to subtract 1 after finding the length of the tuple in Code Box 4.10?

This completes the three-room game where the object is to collect a sim card and a mobile phone.

Adding a story

There is something missing from this adventure, a story!

Will we add one in the next chapter? Will there be a more interesting map? Will the mobile phone ever actually work? Don't miss these and other exciting developments in the next chapter...

Chapter summary

In this chapter you have learnt how to:

- make an infinite game loop
- choose when to use dictionaries, lists and tuples
- create container variables that contain container variables
- create a simple map for an adventure story
- make a simple text-based menu for your app.

Challenge 1

If the player looks in their bag and it is empty, all they currently see is [].
Try to fix this so they see a more helpful message.

Challenge 2

Add a hat stand to the Hall.

Challenge 3

Add a Garden containing a car to the map. Add the Garden so it is before the Reception. Adjust the code so the game starts in the Hall.

Challenge 4

Add a second item, such as a book, to the Lounge and change the code so that the game still works. (For this challenge make the `grab()` function grab everything in the room.)

I am a bit concerned about how a car is going to fit in my backpack ...

Chapter 5
Writing a story

In this chapter you are going to:

- learn even more about dictionaries, lists and tuples

- consider how to program an interactive story

- add a story to your game

- create a simple map for an adventure story.

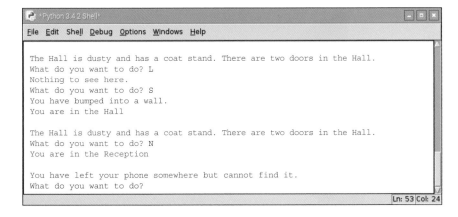

```
The Hall is dusty and has a coat stand. There are two doors in the Hall.
What do you want to do? L
Nothing to see here.
What do you want to do? S
You have bumped into a wall.
You are in the Hall

The Hall is dusty and has a coat stand. There are two doors in the Hall.
What do you want to do? N
You are in the Reception

You have left your phone somewhere but cannot find it.
What do you want to do?
```

Creating an interactive story

Writing a story is a challenge. The author has to keep the reader entertained with a strong plot, great pace, hooks, character development and interesting dialogue. But at least the story in a novel flows from the beginning to the end, which means that the programmer of ebook devices has an easy time of it. In contrast, the old text-based computer adventures had many paths the reader could take and were vast! These were challenging for both the author and the programmer.

You may have read some 'choose your own adventure' books where there are different stories based on the reader's choices: 'If you want to eat the ogre's sandwich turn to paragraph 143.' These also take a lot of care to write and to program.

In Pokémon™ interactive games the player is free to go almost anywhere and chat to almost anyone. The characters say different things at different times in the game. This is the sort of freedom we want for our adventure story app. There are a number of ways of doing this. Here are two possible systems:

Collect items

The player has a selection of items that need to be collected or tasks that need to be performed. The program keeps track of whether the user has done this or not. When a new room is entered the characters and story change dependent on what has been collected or achieved.

Set milestones

In addition to collecting items or doing tasks, at certain milestones all rooms are reset to a new state.

Choosing a system

There are usually several people involved in creating an adventure game. Often the jobs are separated into artists, writers and programmers. A good system should deliver flexibility to the writer and the artist while also being logical to code.

The 'collect items' system is very flexible and relatively easy for the artist but difficult for the writer to keep track of what is going on. It is also difficult for the programmer, especially in a big adventure, because separate logic needs to be written for each room.

The 'set milestones' approach is not quite as flexible but is easier for the writer to organise and for the programmer to code and makes no difference to the artist.

In the rest of this book we are going to use the milestones system. This means we can think of our stories as plays with scenes (rooms), actors (characters) and acts (scenes are reconfigured

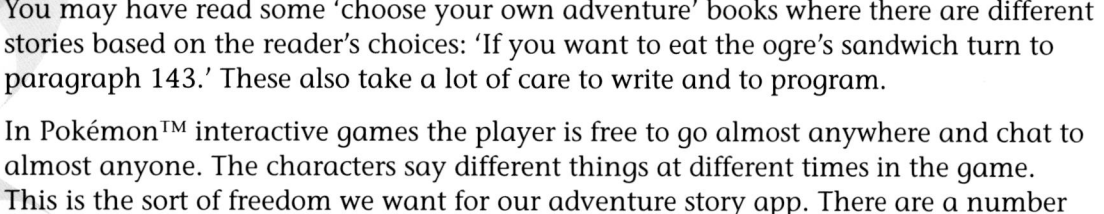

I produced all the images for the adventure in the bonus chapter. I love drawing as well as programming!

after milestones). Finding a familiar model for a complex system is a big advantage as it helps communication between all those involved who are working on it.

Add the story

In this chapter we are going to start at the same point as we left off in Chapter 4 but with a very short story added. This uses a similar structure to rooms. To fit with our drama theme we will call this tuple of dictionaries 'acts'. There are three acts in our story: acts[0], acts[1], acts[2]. The code is shown in Code Box 5.1

The club has done a fantastic job making their adventure game. I hope you enjoy it and, after finishing this book, are inspired to grab some friends and make your own interactive adventure story.

Code Box 5.1

```
# Story divided into three acts each with three scenes
acts = (
    {
        "Reception": "You have left your phone somewhere but cannot find
it.",
        "Hall": "The Hall is dusty and has a coat stand. There are two
doors in the Hall.",
        "Lounge": "This is the Lounge or, as your sister likes to call
it: The No-Reception."
    },
    {
        "Reception": "Your phone does not appear to work.",
        "Hall": "The Hall is dusty and has a coat stand... \nwhich just
stands.",
        "Lounge": "Your phone does not appear to work."
    },
```

(continues on the next page)

```
    {
        "Reception": "Finally, you have a working phone!\nRing ring...\
nRing ring...\n\nPress 'Quit' to finish.",
        "Hall": "You are standing in a Hall with a coat stand... \n...
also standing.",
        "Lounge": "You have a phone with a sim card but still cannot use
it as there is no reception."
    }
)
```

? Quick Quiz 5.1

1 How would you refer to the **string** used in the Reception which reads: "Your phone does not appear to work."?
2 Which string would be returned if your program called acts[2]["Lounge"] ?

This code can be found as rpg3.py in the *Start* folder for this chapter. Open rpg3.py in IDLE and after checking through it, add the extra line of code from Code Box 5.2 to your new **script**.

Code Box 5.2 ✕

```
backpack = []
current_location = 0
act = 0
```

The **variable** act stores the current act we are in. At different milestones it will be advanced to 1 and finally 2.

We need to add two more **functions** to our script: one to check for milestones and update act as required; the other to tell the story. Let's check for milestones first. Add the update_act() function to rpg3.py as shown in Code Box 5.3.

Code Box 5.3

```
# Functions
def update_act():
    global act
    if("mobile phone" in backpack) and ("sim card" in backpack):
        act = 2
    elif "mobile phone" in backpack:
        act = 1
    return act
```

Analysis of Code Box 5.3

The logic for this story is pretty simple. We want to move to Act 1 if the mobile phone is found and to Act 2 if both the sim card and the mobile phone are found, otherwise nothing changes. As nothing changes except in these two circumstances, we do not need an else clause. This function changes the value of the variable act which was **initialised** outside the function, therefore we must re-declare it as a global variable in the function.

Telling the story

The next job is to create the function that tells the story. The first thing it needs to do is check for milestones and find out what act the user is reading. Then it needs to tell the user where they are. (This is better done here than in the game loop now.) Finally it needs to print the appropriate story text for the given room. Add the tell_story() function to rpg3.py just above the update_act() function as shown in Code Box 5.4.

Code Box 5.4 x

```
# Functions
def tell_story():
    update_act()
    room_name = rooms[current_location]["name"]
    print("\nYou are in the " + room_name + "\n")
    print(acts[act][room_name])
```

Finally we need to adjust what happens in the **game loop**. As well as moving, we need to tell the story. We also no longer need to update where the player is in the map as that is done by the story-telling function.

In `rpg3.py`, delete the first line in the game loop and add the two calls to the `tell_story()` function so that your code looks like the code in Code Box 5.5.

Code Box 5.5 x

```
# Create infinite loop
while True:
    command = input("What do you want to do?")
    if command == "L" or command == "l":
        look()
    elif command == "G" or command == "g":
        grab()
    elif command == "I" or command == "i":
        inventory()
    elif command == "N" or command == "n":
        move_north()
```

(continues on the next page)

```
        tell_story()
    elif command == "S" or command == "s":
        move_south()
        tell_story()
    elif command == "Q" or command == "q":
        break
    else:
        print("\nPlease enter only L, G, I, N, S or Q")
```

You have now created a game that functions like a play with acts and scenes (rooms in our case). It also has a simple map and a very simple story that changes depending on which room and which act the player is in. You should now be able to save and run rpg3.py.

Add a more complex map to your game

Most adventure games do not have only three rooms in a row. There are often more complex maps involved, often of vast dungeons or mini worlds. This can get complicated to organise so we need to think of a new system if our game is going to be expandable.

From the *Start* folder open rpg4.py and notice that all mentions of 'rooms' have been changed to 'scenes' to make the whole game more generic. A few new **comments** have been added to indicate where more code will go. To emphasise the need for scenes rather than rooms some new scenes and a new story have been created. Otherwise, this is where you left off with rpg3.py.

As **dictionaries** can have items added to them, there is no need to populate a dictionary initially at all. Thus we can start each game with an empty map and load the scenes into it as required. This makes it much easier to see what is going on.

I am sure I could have come up with a more imaginative story than this! I am having a serious case of déjà vu here.

Add the code from Code Box 5.6 to `rpg4.py` as indicated. Be very careful to get all the commas and other formatting correct. As you type, note how the layout defines a 3×3 map with a **tuple** of three tuples each with three dictionaries! (Note that this script will no longer run for a short while.)

Code Box 5.6

```
# Build the empty map
scenes = (
    ({},{},{}),
    ({},{},{}),
    ({},{},{})
    )
```

Each scene is now represented by a dictionary and the location of each room is found by using a coordinate for the tuple of tuples. See how this works when we load scenes and items into the map. Copy the code from Code Box 5.7 into `rpg4.py` and see how we fill the empty scenes in our map with information for three new locations: `scenes[0][1]`, `scenes[1][1]`, and `scenes[1][2]`.

Code Box 5.7

```
# Load the map with scenes
scenes[0][1]["name"]  = "The Car"
scenes[0][1]["item"]  = "mobile phone"

scenes[1][1]["name"]  = "Yard"

scenes[1][2]["name"]  = "Office"
scenes[1][2]["item"]  = "sim card"
```

This produces a map like this:

0,0	0,1 **The Car** mobile phone	0,2
1,0	1,1 **Yard**	1,2 **Office** sim card
2,0	2,1	2,2

The current location is being stored in a tiny list. This is because although this list currently contains the location of the Reception, as the player moves through the map, the coordinates will have to be updated.

Although this is a simple map, it is now possible to see how easy it is to produce larger maps and keep track of the scenes using a logical coordinate system. It is also easy to add and remove items from scenes.

Before we go any further, you need to change the current_location variable so that instead of storing an integer it stores the starting coordinate [0,1].

When you have finished making these alterations, the beginning of rpg4.py should look like the code shown in Code Box 5.8.

Code Box 5.8

```
# Set global variables
backpack = []
act = 0
current_location = [0,1]
```

(continues on the next page)

```
# Build the empty map

scenes = (
    ({},{},{}),
    ({},{},{}),
    ({},{},{})
    )

# Load the map with scenes
scenes[0][1]["name"] = "The Car"
scenes[0][1]["item"] = "mobile phone"

scenes[1][1]["name"] = "Yard"

scenes[1][2]["name"] = "Office"
scenes[1][2]["item"] = "sim card"
```

Making the app work with the new map

Unfortunately this app will still not work for a little while longer, as we have a few more changes that need to be made. We have to cope with a map where the player can move in four directions instead of two. The app also has to know when the player is trying to move into an empty scene or off the top, bottom or either side of the map. Although we still have a bit of work to do, it is going to be worth it because if we design our code properly, the whole system should work well with any size map and with any number of scenes and acts.

First let's produce a very small function to **return** the current scene. This is best because, although a scene is now defined by simple coordinates, at the moment each scene location is defined by current_location[0] and current_location[1]. This means that the current location becomes rather long and difficult to read. Add the new function get_scene(), shown in Code Box 5.9, just below the update_act() function in rpg4.py.

Code Box 5.9

```
def get_scene():
    return scenes[current_location[0]][current_location[1]]
```

From now on, to find what is at the current coordinates, all we have to do is call `get_scene()`.

This is already required in a number of our functions. To find the current scene in `rpg3.py` we used this snippet of code:

```
scenes[current_location]
```

so before we go any further we should replace all of these with `get_scene()`.

This can easily be achieved by using the find and replace facility in IDLE, accessed by choosing **Replace** from the **Edit** menu. Make sure **wrap around** is selected and then click the **Replace All** button.

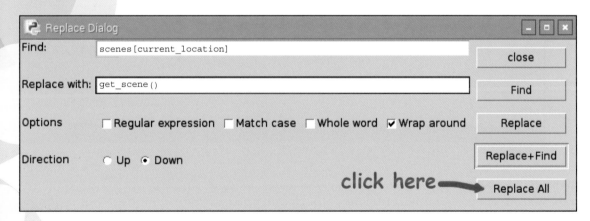

Let's quickly add two functions that test whether the player is trying to go where they shouldn't.

First you will use `get_scene()` to make another function that tests to see if there is a scene loaded into the map at a given location. This function takes advantage of the fact that empty dictionaries, {}, evaluate to `False`. So `get_scene()` tries to return the scene at the current location. If it encounters an empty dictionary the function returns `False`. Our new short function simply reverses this. Add `is_no_scene()` to the bottom of your group of functions as shown in Code Box 5.10.

Code Box 5.10

```
def is_no_scene():
    if get_scene():
        return False
    else:
        return True
```

We also need to know whether the player is trying to move off the map. As the smallest coordinate possible in either direction is 0 and the largest in our 3 x 3 map is 2, we can grab the current x and y coordinates from the `current_location` list and use them to test if the player has gone off the map. Add `is_off_map()` to the growing number of functions in `rpg4.py`. You will find the code in Code Box 5.11.

Code Box 5.11

```
def is_off_map():
    x = current_location[1]
    y = current_location[0]
    if (x < 0) or (x > 2) or (y < 0) or (y > 2):
        return True
    else:
        return False
```

Moving south

The first direction the player wants to head is south so let's make this function work. You will then be able to run `rpg4.py`, at least when heading south! Adjust your south function so that it now looks like the code in Code Box 5.12.

Code Box 5.12

```
def move_south():
    current_location[0] = current_location[0]+1
    if is_off_map() or is_no_scene():
        current_location[0] = current_location[0]-1
        print("You have bumped into a wall.")
```

Analysis of Code Box 5.12

This changes the location by adding 1 to the south coordinate held in `current_location`. It then tests to see if the new location is off the map or in an empty scene. If it finds either of these scenarios to be true, then the function resets the south coordinate back to where it was before and prints a 'wall' message. To remind yourself how the coordinates work, look back at Figure 5.1.

Moving north, east and west

You should now be able to adjust the `move_north()` function so that the player can happily move up and down. Do this and then check everything works as you expect. Moving east or west will not work.

Now use the tried and tested method of 'copy-paste-amend' to create two more functions, `move_east()` and `move_west()`. Then add these two commands to their respective button definitions in the **game loop** at the end of your code to produce a fully working game again.

If you hit any problems, check your code carefully against `rpg4.py` found in the **Finish** folder in this chapter's source code.

This has been a lot of work! And yet all we have done is produce a map without changing the game much from the one in Chapter 4! This hard work has been worth it though. Now it will be easy to add other scenes, items and stories without having to change any of the functions or the code in the game loop.

In the next chapter you will build a **GUI** for the game, which will include the ability to add images to our story. If you have ever played a game on a hand-held console, the interface should look familiar to you.

Chapter summary

In this chapter you have:

- learnt even more about dictionaries, lists and tuples
- considered how to program an interactive story app
- added a story to your game
- created a simple map for an adventure story.

This text-based app is now complete. Here are several challenges.

Challenge 1

Move the Office and sim card from location (1,2) to (1,0). Does the game still just work?

Challenge 2

Add a new scene, such as the Reception, and add some story to accompany it.

Challenge 3

Add a dustbin to the Yard.

Challenge 4

Make the map into a 4 × 4 grid and otherwise change nothing. Does the game still work?

Challenge 5

Make the map into a 2 × 2 grid and tuck the scenes into it.

Idea

Write your own old-school adventure and find someone your parent's age to enjoy it! They will be very impressed.

Chapter 6
An adventure game console

In this chapter you are going to:

- build a GUI for your game

- learn more about arranging tkinter widgets in frames.

> I hope you like my drawings! Of course you can easily replace mine with your own to give a completely different feel to your own adventures.

Building our GUI

In this chapter we are going to build a simple **tkinter** interface for our story-telling app.

Instead of having to hit the N, S, E and W keys we will add arrow buttons. We will then not need to supply a menu as these buttons are intuitive.

Instead of typing L, I and G we will provide buttons with obvious icons. We will also provide a Quit button to close the window and release resources back to **IDLE**.

These are all buttons that need to be arranged nicely so we will use tkinter frames to place them.

In addition, we will add a textbox to display our story text and a canvas on which to display images of our scenes, which will help to orientate the players.

A lot of this is similar to the ebook we made in Chapter 3 although the buttons now have images and we are adding a canvas **widget**.

Organising the project

Look in the **Start** folder in the **Chapter6** folder of the source code. Here you will find a Python **script** called `rpg-gui.py` and an images folder containing all the images you will need. Have a look at the images and see how they match the design shown on the first page of this chapter.

Open `rpg-gui.py` in IDLE and notice that there are **comments** indicating where everything should go from Chapter 5 and some placeholder **functions** ready for the buttons so that we do not crash the application every time we press a button. Instead of our game loop we are going to use tkinter's. At the beginning of the script you will find five configuration type variables. In this chapter you are only going to add code to the `main` section of this script.

Organising the frames

This app uses several frames. The first is the top one to hold the canvas and text area. There are three more to hold the groups of buttons. They are all built in a similar way so you can add them to `rpg-gui.py` all at once by typing in the code from Code Box 6.1. You will find out if you have made any mistakes when the buttons are added!

Code Box 6.1   x

```
# Create top frame
topframe = Frame(window)
topframe.grid(row=0, column=0, columnspan=3, sticky=N)

# Create bottom_left frame
bottom_left = Frame(window)
bottom_left.grid(row=1, column=0, sticky=NW)
```

(continues on the next page)

```
# Create bottom_centre frame
bottom_centre = Frame(window)
bottom_centre.grid(row=1, column=1, sticky=N)

# Create bottom_right frame
bottom_right = Frame(window)
bottom_right.grid(row=1, column=2, sticky=NE)
```

Importing images

Eight images are used in the GUI and there is one more image for testing purposes. The images have to be imported and assigned variable names so we can refer to them when we want to use them. To do this we use tkinter's PhotoImage() function. Add the code from Code Box 6.2 to rpg-gui.py now.

Code Box 6.2

```
# Load images for scenes
car = PhotoImage(file="images/scene_car.gif")

# Load images for move buttons
up = PhotoImage(file="images/up.gif")
left = PhotoImage(file="images/left.gif")
right = PhotoImage(file="images/right.gif")
down = PhotoImage(file="images/down.gif")

# Load images for bottom buttons
bag = PhotoImage(file="images/backpack.gif")
grabber = PhotoImage(file="images/grab.gif")
search = PhotoImage(file="images/look.gif")
quit_image = PhotoImage(file="images/quit.gif")
```

Notice how the image file name and the path to it (they are all in the images folder) are passed to the `PhotoImage()` function as a **string**.

Add a scene image

First add a canvas widget by copying in the code from Code Box 6.3.

```
Code Box 6.3                                                    x

# Setup canvas
canvas = Canvas(topframe, height=canvas_height,
                width=canvas_width, highlightthickness=0)
canvas.grid(row=0,column=0)
```

Note how we have used variables to hold the width and height so that we can adjust them at the top of the script if we want to. `highlightthickness=0` is an optional **argument** that makes the canvas sit against the containing frame with no border.

Just above the `mainloop()` we will add the car scene image. This is placed in the game section as this is where the scenery will be changed in the final app. Add the code from Code Box 6.4 to your script.

```
Code Box 6.4                                                    x

# Start game
canvas.create_image(0, 0, image=car, anchor=NW)
```

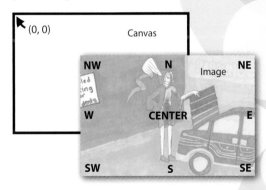

The first two arguments (`0, 0`) indicate where on the canvas the image is to be placed, in this case, the top left corner of the canvas. However by **default** it is the centre of the image that is placed there so we need to indicate that we want the anchor point for our image to be the top left corner of the image – its north-west corner.

Playing with the canvas

Try the following experiments to get the hang of how the canvas widget works:

1 Delete `highlightthickness=0` from your code where you created the canvas and try running the script. (Put it back again afterwards.)
2 Delete `anchor=NW` from your code where you added the image and try running the script. Remember that by default the centre of the image is placed at 0,0 on the canvas.
3 Try changing `anchor=NW` to `anchor=N` and running the script. Note how the middle top of the image is now at coordinate 0,0 on the canvas.
4 Try changing the coordinates of the canvas so the image is positioned at 300,200 (the centre of the canvas). Which of the allowed anchor points is now required to place the image where it should be? The allowed anchor points are N, S, E, W, NW, NE, SW, SE and CENTER.

Before continuing make sure you put this line of code back to how it was in Code Box 6.4.

Add a textbox

The process of adding a textbox is similar to adding the canvas. First add a textbox widget and then add some text to check it works. To make it look nice we give this widget its own background colour. Amend `rpg-gui.py` so that your code matches that in Code Boxes 6.5 and 6.6.

Code Box 6.5

```
# Build story area
story_box = Text(topframe, height=text_box_height,
                 width=text_box_width, background=paper_colour)
story_box.grid(row=1, column=0)
```

Code Box 6.6

```
# Start game
canvas.create_image(0, 0, image=car, anchor=NW)
story_box.insert(END, "text goes here")
```

> I remember this from Chapter 3. END tells the insert() method to put the text at the end of any text that is already in the textbox but as there isn't any, this means at the beginning!!

Adding all the buttons

You are now going to add all the direction buttons into the `bottom_right` frame. These are all positioned by placing them in their own cells within the frame. Copy in the required code from Code Box 6.7 and then run the file to check all is OK before proceeding.

Code Box 6.7

```
# Direction buttons
Button(bottom_right, image=up, command=move_north).grid(row=0, column=2)
Button(bottom_right, image=left, command=move_west).grid(row=1, column=1)
Button(bottom_right, image=right, command=move_east).grid(row=1, column=3)
Button(bottom_right, image=down, command=move_south).grid(row=2, column=2)
```

As we are not going to refer to them in the rest of our script, we do not need to assign each button a variable name.

You can now add the rest of the buttons to the other two frames. Think about how the positioning works as you type in the code from Code Box 6.8.

Code Box 6.8

```
# Other buttons
Button(bottom_centre, image=search, command=look).grid(row=0, column=0)
Button(bottom_centre, image=bag, command=inventory).grid(row=0, column=1)
Button(bottom_centre, image=grabber, command=grab).grid(row=0, column=2)
Button(bottom_left, image=quit_image, command=quit_game).grid()
```

That completes the GUI. The only button that works is Quit.

Creating the GUI has not been very difficult because adding widgets with tkinter is quite easy once you get the hang of it. You are now in a position to make all sorts of professional looking apps!

Chapter summary

In this chapter you have:

- learnt how to build a GUI for your game
- learnt more about arranging tkinter widgets in frames.

Challenge 1

Swap the Quit button with the arrow buttons.

Challenge 2

Replace the tkinter textbox widget with a scrolling text widget. (There are short recipes for the tkinter widgets in the Appendix.)

Idea

Make your own button images and substitute them for the ones supplied.

Chapter 7
A mysterious mystery

In this chapter you are going to:

- add the story to the GUI

- think about how to divide up tasks.

The joy of team work

This project produces quite a long Python **script**. By working on separate parts it is possible to get more than one person involved. For example, you could sit down with your friends and decide how the **GUI** will look, then one person could go and code this separately (like we did in Chapter 6), another small team could work on the story, and a couple of friends could work on the images, while another small group could code all of the **functions** ready to be attached to the GUI.

Whether working in a team or on your own, breaking up projects into smaller tasks makes producing something ambitious manageable. The functions you created for the earlier simple text-based game will make a very good starting point for our GUI app.

The final leg
Merging two files

Look in the **Start** folder in the **Chapter7** folder of the source code. Here you will find the two Python scripts from the previous two chapters, called `rpg-gui.py` and `rpg4.py`, together with an images folder containing all the images you will need.

Open `rpg-gui.py` in **IDLE** and look at it to remind yourself about the comments indicating where the functions should go. Now open `rpg4.py` next to it ready to start merging the contents. You are going to use `rpg-gui.py` as the target script and copy from `rpg4.py`.

See if you can join these two files by following this checklist:

1 Copy across the global variables.
2 Copy across the empty map `scenes`.
3 Copy across the code that loads the scenes.
4 Copy across the `acts` tuple of dictionaries with the story text.
5 Copy across the three missing functions: `tell_story()`, `update_act()` and `get_scene()`.
6 Replace `pass` in all the functions in `rpg-gui.py` with the code in the function with the same name from `rpg4.py`.
7 Copy across the last two missing functions: `is_off_map()` and `is_no_scene()`.

When this is complete you can check your code by running it. It should produce the same GUI as before and a few of the buttons will produce some text in the Python shell.

If there is a problem, there is a copy of this joined file in the **Extras** folder called `rpg-joined.py`. You can compare this script with yours to see if you have missed something.

Transferring the story to the textbox

Whenever we change scene, the app is going to call the `tell_story()` function. The first thing we want to happen here is for any text that is already there to be deleted. To do this we use tkinter's `delete()` **method**. This takes two arguments, where to delete from and where to delete to. We are going to delete all of the text so the second **argument** needs to be END (which you have met before). The first argument needs to represent the beginning of the text. The argument has to be a coordinate supplied as a **string**. It takes the form `"1.0"` where 1 represents the first row of text and the 0 indicates the cursor position in front of the first character. Add the code from Code Box 7.1 to the top of the `tell_story()` function just above `update_act()`.

Code Box 7.1

```
def tell_story():
    # clear story box
    story_box.delete("1.0", END)
```

Delving Deeper

tkinter documentation

It is not difficult to find out how all of tkinter's methods work and what arguments are required to make them behave in the way you intend. All you need to do is look up the documentation. A search such as 'tkinter documentation Python 3' should be fruitful and will probably take you here:

https://docs.python.org/3/library/tkinter.html

At the time of writing, this page has rather a lot of information and background about **tkinter** but it also recommends a few friendlier sites including:

http://infohost.nmt.edu/tcc/pubs/tkinter/web/

This is a well-indexed and easy-to-navigate site. You should be able to find any information you need here.

Don't forget that there are also some quick reminders collected together in the Appendix.

Now, instead of printing everything to the Python **shell**, we need to load all our messages into a variable ready to add to `story_box`. We will use a **local variable** in all our functions and, as it is a local variable, we can use the same name all the time. We will call it `msg`.

We can make some use of IDLE's ability to find and replace text to help with this task. From the *Edit* menu select *Replace*. Then search for `'print('` and replace it with `'msg = '` and click *Replace all*. This nearly completes the job for us but we need to remove the trailing bracket from all the `print()` statements so scroll through your file and wherever you see `msg` look for the extra bracket at the end of the line of code and delete it leaving the final speech mark. Here is an example of before and after:

Before:

```
print("You are in the " + get_scene()["name"] + "\n")
```

After find and replace:

```
msg = "You are in the " + get_scene()["name"] + "\n")
```

After removal of the trailing bracket:

```
msg = "You are in the " + get_scene()["name"] + "\n"
```

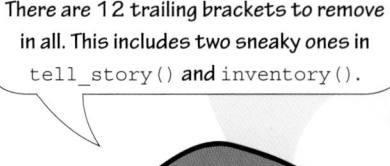

There are 12 trailing brackets to remove in all. This includes two sneaky ones in `tell_story()` and `inventory()`.

After removing all the trailing brackets, the next task is to add the code that inserts the messages in the textbox. This can be achieved with the same line of code added directly after each `msg` line (or at the end of the function if there is an `if` clause). The line of code is shown in Code Box 7.2 and you can add it now. There is no need to amend the `tell_story()` function as this will be amended a bit later. You can check you completed this process properly by looking at the highlighted code in Code Box 7.3.

Code Box 7.2

```
story_box.insert(END, msg)
```

```python
def look():
    if "item" in get_scene():
        msg = "You can see a " + get_scene["item"]
    else:
        msg = "Nothing to see here."
    story_box.insert(END, msg)
def grab():
    if "item" in get_scene():
        backpack.append(get_scene()["item"])
        msg = "You now have the " + get_scene["item"]
        del get_scene()["item"]
    else:
        msg = "Nothing to grab here."
    story_box.insert(END, msg)
def inventory():
    if len(backpack) != 0:
        msg = backpack
    else:
        msg = "You have not collected anything yet."
    story_box.insert(END, msg)
def quit_game():
    window.withdraw()
    window.quit()
```

(continues on the next page)

```
def move_north():
    current_location[0] = current_location[0]-1
    if is_off_map() or is_no_scene():
        current_location[0] = current_location[0]+1
        msg = "You have bumped into a wall."
        story_box.insert(END, msg)

def move_south():
    current_location[0] = current_location[0]+1
    if is_off_map() or is_no_scene():
        current_location[0] = current_location[0]-1
        msg = "You have bumped into a wall."
        story_box.insert(END, msg)

def move_east():
    current_location[1] = current_location[1]+1
    if is_off_map() or is_no_scene():
        current_location[1] = current_location[1]-1
        msg = "You have bumped into a wall."
        story_box.insert(END, msg)

def move_west():
    current_location[1] = current_location[1]-1
    if is_off_map() or is_no_scene():
        current_location[1] = current_location[1]+1
        msg = "You have bumped into a wall."
        story_box.insert(END, msg)
```

Your script will still run, to an extent. If you try it you will see that there is a little tweaking necessary before we can deal with the `tell_story()` function.

A little tweaking

First there is a little problem to sort out with the `inventory()` function. Just printing out the contents of `backpack` seems a bit odd in this context. It would be better to build a more readable **string**. Because `backpack` is not a string we cannot simply add it to another string. This is resolved by **casting** `backpack` to a string. Amend `inventory()` now with the help of Code Box 7.4.

Code Box 7.4

```
def inventory():
    if len(backpack) != 0:
        msg = "Your bag contains: " + str(backpack)
    else:
        msg = "You have not collected anything yet."
    story_box.insert(END, msg)
```

Did you know dedent is the opposite of indent? Dedent is currently my favourite word but it is very difficult to use in everyday life – I know because I have tried!

Delving Deeper

Indenting and dedenting

In Python, the preferred distance to indent a block of code is four spaces. Sometimes when wrapping a block of code in a new if statement or moving a block of code into a function, several lines have to be indented. It is also often necessary to remove indentation. These two processes can be done manually by repeatedly pressing the space bar or the delete key. However, there is an easier way:

To indent a block of code in IDLE:
Highlight the lines of code to be indented and then choose **Indent Region** from the **Format** menu.

To dedent a block of code in IDLE:
Highlight the lines of code to be dedented and then choose **Dedent Region** from the **Format** menu.

Another new problem is that because the **script** does not empty the text box unless we change scene, the messages all pile up when the player is looking or grabbing, and so on. It would be best to put every message on a new line, to make your app appear a little more professional. All you have to do is add \n at the beginning of every `msg` string highlighted in Code Box 7.3. For example in `move_west()`, `msg` becomes:

```
msg = "\nYou have bumped into a wall."
```

Go through the functions `look()`, `grab()`, `inventory()`, `move_north()`, `move_south()`, `move_east()` and `move_west()` and add \n to every `msg` string now.

Telling the story

You have now completed the combining of the two scripts produced earlier in this project (the GUI script and the text-based script) and tweaked things a little. Now we need to finish the app.

First, let's add the scenery. Because this uses tkinter's `PhotoImage()` function, this has to be done between `window = Tk()` and `window.mainloop()`. The process for adding an image is: first load the image using `PhotoImage()`, then assign it to a **variable**, and finally add the image variable to the map. This is the same process we went through at the top of the script with the items and the scenery names.

There are three images to add. You can do this now by copying the code from Code Box 7.5 into your copy of `rpg_gui.py`. As you do so, note how your dictionaries in the scenes map can easily hold a mixture of **strings** and image objects. The **container data types** in Python are very flexible.

Code Box 7.5

```
# Load and assign images for scenes
car = PhotoImage(file="images/scene_car.gif")
scenes[0][1]["image"] = car

outside = PhotoImage(file="images/scene_outside.gif")
scenes[1][1]["image"] = outside

office = PhotoImage(file="images/scene_office.gif")
scenes[1][2]["image"] = office
```

Now we are ready to tell our story. To start the game we want to load the image for the first scene and then call `tell_story()`. Adjust the code to do this by replacing the placeholder code from the GUI design process with the code in Code Box 7.6. (This code is found nearly at the end of the script.)

Code Box 7.6

```
# Start game
canvas.create_image(0, 0, image=car, anchor=NW)
tell_story()
```

Having loaded everything and set up a start image and a start location, all we need to do is to call the `tell_story()` function every time we move scenes. It will handle scene changes and selecting the story text for whichever scene or act we are in. So your final task is to adjust `tell_story()`. Do this now by amending your current code to match that in Code Box 7.7. Notice how much you understand as you type it in. A brief analysis follows this code box.

Code Box 7.7

```python
def tell_story():
    # load the scenery
    canvas.create_image(0, 0, image=get_scene()["image"], anchor=NW)
    # clear the story box
    story_box.delete("1.0", END)

    update_act()

    # build the story
    msg = "You are in the " + get_scene()["name"] + "\n"
    msg = msg + acts[act][get_scene()["name"]]
    story_box.insert(END, msg)
```

Analysis of Code Box 7.7

This is not very difficult to understand: you have already studied how to add images to tkinter's canvas. You know how the `delete()` **method** works from earlier in this chapter. `update_act()` calls the `update_act()` function which was built some time ago as a simple helper function. You are also familiar now with how to insert a string (in this case `msg`) into the story box with tkinter's `insert()` method. That leaves the building of the story and storing it in `msg`.

The story is built in two parts. First the string is created to tell the player where they are and then a carriage return is added. The interesting stuff happens in the next line: `acts[act][get_scene()["name"]]` is added to the end of the string already stored in `msg`.

Expert Challenge

If you like a challenge you should see if you can work out what string
`acts[act][get_scene()["name"]]` generates in the very first scene
of the game. If you can do this, you can count yourself a true Python
container variable expert!

The answer follows below.

This is what this small line of code does in the very first scene: `get_scene()`
finds the current coordinates stored in `current_location`. At the beginning
of the game these are `0` and `1`. Therefore `get_scene()["name"]` equates
to `scenes[0][1]["name"]` which is the string `"The Car"`. So now this small
chunk of code equates to `acts[act]["The Car"]`. At the beginning
of the game, **act** is 0. So in the very first scene of the game:

`acts[act][get_scene()["name"]]` equates to `acts[0]["The Car"]`

This is, of course, the string:

`"You have left your phone somewhere but cannot find it.\nHow annoying :-(".`

One final thing

All our move functions not only have to move the player into a new room, they
should also call the `tell_story()` method. Code Box 7.8 shows how to add this to
`move_north()`.

Amend this function in your script now and then do the same for the other three move functions.

Code Box 7.8

```
def move_north():
    current_location[0] = current_location[0]-1
    if is_off_map() or is_no_scene():
        current_location[0] = current_location[0]+1
        msg = "\nYou have bumped into a wall."
        story_box.insert(END, msg)
    else:
        tell_story()
```

This completes the app. You can now save your file, run it and enjoy this rather too familiar adventure!

Chapter summary

In this chapter you have learnt how to:

- add the story to the GUI
- think about how to divide up tasks.

The app is now complete, so here are a few ideas for **hacking** it:

Ideas

- Use the app and note down what you like and do not like.
- Draw your own scenes and use them to replace those supplied.
- Extend the map, add more rooms, items and change the story.
- If you want longer stories, replace the text box with a ScrolledText box.

Challenge 1

Move the Quit button to the centre and add a set of four A, B, C, D buttons that mirror the arrow buttons as shown:

Don't forget to supply placeholder functions for them to call.

Challenge 2

Add a global variable called `max_backpack_content` and set its value to `1`. Add some code to the `grab()` function to detect whether the backpack is full and provide an appropriate message. (This script is used in the next challenge.)

Challenge 3

To the script you produced in Challenge 2, add an item to the Yard called 'big bag'. Then add some code to the `grab()` function to detect when the big bag is grabbed and increase the maximum number of items the player can carry to `three`.

Bonus material

In the **Chapter7** folder in the source code, downloaded from the companion website, you will find a **Bonus** folder. This has a complete adventure story named `mysteriousMystery.py`. The Coding Club members have worked hard on this and enjoyed producing all the resources, which you are free to use.

All Coding Club books provide at least one bonus application for you to examine and figure out what is going on. This is an important skill to develop. `mysteriousMystery.py` provides you with quite a few new functions that you might want to include in your own applications.

We suggest you play our game and enjoy it before looking at the notes below.

Notes for the Mysterious Mystery app

Stage directions

The bonus application has been written in a slightly different way to `rpg_gui.py` because there is more than one line of text per scene in each act. The application is now very much like a play with characters and a dialogue-driven plot. To facilitate team work, the application can now take stage directions that are added in the story. This should make life much easier for the script writers (although they must still stick rigidly to the nested container structure).

The programmer has worked a bit harder to make this possible with a new `stage_directions()` function that looks through the dialogue strings for the stage directions and then handles them.

Characters and items

Characters and items in the story now show up in scenes. This is handled by the stage directions ADD, ENTER and EXIT.

Sound

Sound effects (SFX) and background music are implemented in this app. This is provided by `simpleAudio.py`, which must be in the same folder as the application. This module has to handle the fact that different operating systems provide sound resources in different ways. Note that it is imported in a different way to the `tkinter module`. This is in line with recommended Python practice that only one module should be imported with the `from` keyword. When you import with `from` it is not necessary to precede methods with the module name followed by a point, (in this case, `tkinter.`). However, it also means that it is difficult to tell where the methods have come from. Because of the way it is imported, calls to the methods in the `simpleAudio` module are obvious because they have to start with `simpleAudio.`

The script, which was written by David Kosbie, is freely available on the internet.

The move functions

You may wish to look at how the move functions have been **refactored** by pulling out the common code into a separate `move()` function.

Image dictionary

Do you remember how we needed to import some of our images in `rpg_gui.py` into the tkinter area of the script? This application tries to avoid this so that all the images can be amended in the same place. Unfortunately to enable the stage directions function to work we have to be able to map a text name for the images to their actual variable name. This is what the `image_dictionary` does.

Bonus ideas

I hope you can see that there are lots of possibilities here. You could make your own cool story-telling app with changing images in each scene by hacking `rpg_gui.py` and providing a more exciting story of your own. You could add one or two of the facilities from `mysteriousMystery.py`.

Alternatively if you can get a group of friends or a class of students together, you can produce new backdrops, items and characters of your own, write a new play and turn it into an exciting app by hacking the top section of `mysteriousMystery.py`.

I hope you enjoyed our murder mystery adventure story as much as we enjoyed making it!

Appendix

Some key bits of information

The companion website

Website: www.codingclub.co.uk

The companion website has the answers to the puzzles and challenges in the book and the complete source code including start files and the bonus code. You will also find information about other books in the series, character profiles, and much, much more.

Black Flag website

Website: www.cambridge.org/codingclub-blackflag

The companion website to the Coding Club novel, *Black Flag*, has lots of extra puzzles and challenges for you to complete. Can you help Cal on his quest to defeat the shadowy group known as the Anarchists?

Container data type summary

The table below assumes these data structures have been created:

```
>>> s = "bar" # a string
>>> t = ("b", "a", "r") # a tuple
>>> l = ["b", "a", "r"] # a list
>>> d = {1:"b", 2:"a", 3:"r"} # a dictionary
```

This table provides a list of useful functions that you can use on these data types.

Method	Strings	Tuples	Lists	Dictionaries
Print all	`>>> print(s)` `bar`	`>>> print(t)` `('b', 'a', 'r')`	`>>> print(l)` `['b', 'a', 'r']`	`>>> print(d)` `{1: 'b', 2: 'a', 3:`
Print element	`>>> print(s[2])` `r`	`>>> print(t[2])` `r`	`>>> print(l[2])` `r`	`>>> print(d[2])` `a`

Combine	`>>> a=s+"f"`
	`>>> a`
	`'barf'`
		`>>> a=t+("f",)`
		`>>> a`
		`('b', 'a', 'r', 'f')`
			`>>> a=l+["f"]`
			`>>> a`
			`['b', 'a', 'r', 'f']`	

Add an element			`>>> l.append("f")`
			`>>> l`
			`['b', 'a', 'r', 'f']`
				`>>> d[4]="f"`
				`>>> d[4]`
				`'f'`

Sort			`>>> l.sort()`
			`>>> l`
			`['a', 'b', 'r']`
				`>>> sorted(d)`
				`['1', '2', '3']`
				`>>> sorted(d.values`
				`['a', 'b', 'r']`

Delete an element			`>>> del l[1]`
			`>>> l`
			`['b', 'r']`
				`>>> del d[1]`
				`>>> i`
				`{2:'a', 3:'r'}`

Replace element			`>>> l[0]="c"`
			`>>> l`
			`['c', 'a', 'r']`
				`>>> d[1]="c"`
				`>>> print(d)`
				`{1: 'c', 2: 'a', 3:`

Find	`>>> i.find("b")` `0`	`>>> t.index("b")` `0`	`>>> l.index("b")` `0`	
Get length	`>>> len(s)` `3`	`>>> len(t)` `3`	`>>> len(l)` `3`	`>>> len(d)` `3`

Some useful tkinter widgets

Code to create an empty window ready for widgets:

```python
from tkinter import *
# Create a window and add a title:
window = Tk()
window.title("My application")

# Code for tkinter widgets goes here #

# Start tkinter's loop which watches for changes:
window.mainloop()
```

The code for some tkinter widgets:

```python
my_frame = Frame(window, height=50, width=100, bg="green")

my_label = Label(my_frame, text="My text goes here")

my_text_entry_box = Entry(my_frame, width=20, bg="light green")

my_button = Button(my_frame, text="SUBMIT", width=5,
                   command=function_name_to_be_called)

my_text_box = Text(my_frame, width=75, height=6, wrap=WORD,
                   background="light green")
```

A recipe for providing a drop-down menu tkinter widget:

```
options = (1,2,3)
var = IntVar() # value accessed with var.get()
var.set("choose:")
my_dropdown = OptionMenu(window, var, *options)
my_dropdown.grid()
```

Creating an infinite loop

```
while True:
    # Code that repeats forever goes here
```

Catching errors

```
def my_function(args):
    try:
        # your code goes here
    except:
        return "--> Error!"
```

Glossary

algorithm	step-by-step instructions to perform a task that a computer can understand	25
argument	a piece of information that is required by a function so that it can perform its task, usually a string or number: `my_function(arguments go here)`	38
ASCII	stands for American Standard Code for Information Interchange; it contains 128 characters and does not include special characters such as those with accents	39
casting	the process of converting one data type into another; e.g. sometimes a number is stored as text but may need to be converted into an integer – this can be done like this: `int("3")`	25
commenting	some text in a computer program that is for the human reader and is ignored by the computer when running the program – in Python all comments begin with a hash symbol #	32
container	container data types store groups of other data types, which may include more containers; the containers used in this book are **tuples**, **lists** and **dictionaries**	7
data type	different types of information stored by the computer, for example floats, integers, strings, tuples, lists and dictionaries	7
decomposition	an important computational thinking skill which involves breaking complex tasks into smaller simpler ones	31
default	a value given to an argument as a starting point when writing a function or method	77

infinite loop	a piece of code that keeps running forever – usually a bad thing, but not always	46
integer	a number data type that cannot have a decimal value and must be a whole number	7
interactive mode	this is when we use IDLE to try out snippets of code in Python's **shell** without saving	13
initialise	to give a newly created variable a value	50
iteration	the process of looping through a sequence of code	26
key	the equivalent of an index for a string, tuple or list but for a dictionary; it is defined by the programmer and can, for example, be a string, integer, float or even a tuple, in a `key:value` pair	14
list	an ordered container data type that can hold values of any type and can have elements added or removed; like tuples, each element is indexed from `0`	13
local variable	a variable that is defined inside a function and is only usable inside that function	55
loop	a piece of code that keeps repeating until a certain condition is met	13
method	the name given to a function in a class	12
module	a saved Python file whose functions can be used by another program	9
modulus	a mathematical **operator** that is used to return the remainder from a division calculation, e.g. `22%7` returns `1`	28

operator	a symbol that performs a simple function on some code such as multiplying two numbers or comparing them to see if they are equal	12
ordered container	a container data type in which the values stored are indexed together with their position in the container, e.g. **tuples** and **lists**; a **dictionary** is an example of an unordered container	16
output	data that is sent from a program to a screen or printer etc	
refactoring	the process of changing the structure of code so it is less repetitive, more readable, easier to maintain, and so on	95
return	(1) the value a function produces when it is run – it is also a Python keyword; (2) the 'end of line' key on a keyboard, sometimes called the enter key	13
script	the name given to Python program files; these end in .py	10
script mode	this is when we use **IDLE** to help us write code that we will save in a file, or **script**	10
shell	the first window that opens when **IDLE** is started; it is great for trying out short snippets of code in interactive sessions; when running scripts it acts as a console where print statements and error messages appear and where users can provide input	14
statement	a snippet of code; strictly speaking it is a piece of code that represents a command or action. e.g. a print statement	12
string	text data that can be stored in a variable	7
tkinter	a package of classes often imported into Python programs that provide methods that are useful for producing windows, drawing images and producing animations	32

tuple	an ordered **container** data type whose values are indexed from 0; its contents cannot be changed	7
value	anything that can be stored in a **variable** such as the elements in a **container** data type	8
variable	a name that refers to a place in a computer's memory where data is stored; more loosely, it can also be used to refer to that data	12
while loop	a kind of loop that repeats code while a comparative statement returns `True`	13
widget	an element of a GUI such as a button or text entry box	32

The Quick Quiz answers

Quick Quiz 1.1

4 The seven of hearts.

Quick Quiz 1.2

```
my_random_rank = rank[random.randint(0,12)]
```

Quick Quiz 1.3

```
"three of diamonds"
```

Quick Quiz 1.4

1 a tuple
2 a list
3 a tuple

Quick Quiz 1.5

1 a dictionary
2 a tuple
3 a list
4 a list

Quick Quiz 4.1

This depends entirely on how the rooms are going to be used, so this is perhaps an unfair question. However, it is one that the programmer needs to answer at the planning stage. In the current situation a tuple is a good choice if the number of dictionaries is not going to change. Surprisingly, if the contents of a dictionary changes within a tuple this does not count as a change to the tuple (which, of course, cannot change) This is because the tuple is just storing a reference to the dictionaries.

Quick Quiz 4.2

The length of the rooms tuple is 3 because there are three rooms. However, containers are indexed from zero so, to find the correct index, we have to subtract 1 from the length.

Quick Quiz 5.1

1 `acts[1]["Reception"]`
2 "You have a phone with a sim card but still cannot use it as there is no reception."

Acknowledgements

One of the themes in this book is teamwork. I am very lucky to have great editors, copy-editors, proof readers, artists and designers helping me when writing my books. Thanks, as always, go to Alex and everyone at Cambridge University Press. Working with a talented team is a very fulfilling experience. Thanks also to David Kosbie for allowing me (and you the readers) to use his great little simpleAudio.py script in our apps.

This book required a lot of extra images to make the final adventures more interesting. I am immensely grateful to Kaia, the newest member of the team, for her fantastic pictures that add so much to the "Mysterious Mystery".

I cannot thank Rita, Joe and Dan enough for their help, support and forebearance with my "projects". I have a fantastic family!